dancing with death
Reflections from a Student of Pain

By Elayna Fernández ~ The Positive MOM

Dancing with Death
Reflections from a Student of Pain
By Elayna Fernández ~ The Positive MOM

Book cover design by Elisha Fernández.

Published by thePositiveMOM.com
ISBN: 978-1-952201-29-5

To Elisha, my firstborn
and partner in poetry.

On Dancing and Dying

Storytelling Poetry

———

I've often found myself between three wishes: wishing I were dead, wishing I felt truly alive, and wishing for the dance between these two to go away.

I used to fill my spirit with guilt, shame, and regret because the dance would not stop. And only one-hundred-percent of the time, the pain would not go away... It would only grow more intense.

It wasn't until I stopped wishing my struggles away with toxic positivity, that I was able to find beauty, learning, and peace in my pain.

My dance with death has given room for celebration in life.

The twenty-one poems you are about to read represent transformed pain. It is my wish that they inspire you to invite your pain to emerge, so it can turn into art.

Each poem tells a story of my life, sometimes one I've lived a thousand times. At the end of each poem, I've included my reflection and space for your own reflection, and perhaps, your own story.

I invite you on a journey to become a Student of Pain, loving both your inner light and the shadows that are created when your luminous Self is blocked in this life experience.

Blessings,

Elayna

preview

———

the verse

end the sentence
and savor the sweet taste of freedom
feel the sweet release
escape this prison
use the period
make it go away

scared of question marks
exhausted by pleads and exclamations
to be seen, to be heard,
and understood
to be enough
and not feel like a burden

they'll gather up
celebrate and mourn my dash
and then move on
to their next paragraph
as I enjoy the silence of the blank page
a new start without pain

when my fragile body dies
it will stop aching, but
when my heart stops
will it stop breaking?
is the period enough
to make it stop?

guilt for a Capital Sin
a lower case of nostalgia
for what could have been
the question marks stab at me
but I couldn't ask someone else
it's not grammatically correct

is it cheating if I ask for help?
I do because it may give meaning to this test...
his words help me connect the dots
and cheat death
I'm not using a full stop this time
I'll use a semicolon instead.

This is a recurrent story in my life. I remember it playing in my head well before my fifth birthday. Asking for help can feel like the most impossible thing to do when we are battling with suicidal thoughts, but it's really the easiest way out. Even when it feels that there's no safe place or person, we can call a helpline: 800-273-8255.

What are your thoughts on suicidal ideation and asking for help?

_____

_____

_____

_____

_____

_____

_____

_____

_____

_____

two left feet

put my hair in a bun

"Wear comfy shoes
go dance your song"

Earth awaits
slip on a twirly dress
and cross the gates

but I'm an infant
my feet don't work
not in an instant

I hear the beat
it's calling me
but seems I've got useless feet

I crawl through life
but why oh why
I came to dance, not to strive

I know there's more
I don't want to crawl
I want to shine on the dance floor

I'm stepping up
I walk at last
is it too slow, is it too fast

dancing with death

never enough
I want to run
be like the others, forget the song

my soul keeps calling
but I'm afraid
will I end up stumbling and falling?
watch your step, fix your form
you're a dancer now
you must conform

obsessed with a perfection
dancing in the dark
no sense of direction

judged with precision
tired, sweaty, thrusting
dancing someone else's song - was it my
decision?

I yearn to hear them clap
but they couldn't care less
it's the end, it's a wrap

bare feet, high heels, pointe shoes
I want twirls, I want leaps
I want to choose

a step forward, a step back
ugly cacophony
but I know I'm on track

dancing with death

raggedy dress, flawed bun
earth is no place
for comfort zones

the music stops
It's dark once more
I'm all alone on the dance floor

be still and listen
it's a symphony
spin and jump and dance carefree

my song comes on
what a thrilling beat
but now I've aged and have two left feet

Life can feel like a journey of inadequacy...

This is my story of feeling like I'm never where I want to be, like I don't belong, and I'll never fit in. I've lived this story when I'm focused on comparison and obsessed with meeting impossible standards of perfection.

Can you relate? What is your story of striving?

_____

_____

_____

_____

_____

_____

_____

_____

_____

_____

trip to the light

sitting in a dark room
critiquing my own performance
a review of an unlived life

it's cold, it's scary
trapped
can't move my feet

the floor quakes
my soul sways
my lifeless body remains

I wander in a bright ballroom
doors everywhere
but I don't want to escape

open windows
open truth
light and peaceful solitude

yellow space, purple souls
celestial dancers greet me
finally free to leap

regrets forgiven
pain understood
wrongs righted in a whirl of truth

enlightened consciousness
light years
only the hum of Love and warmth

heavenly messenger
says "one more dance"
choraphobia strikes once again

bright lights flicker
hesitant to return
to fiddle around on planet Earth

stunning sights, sounds of harps
deep connection
to love Divine

angelic choirs
warmth and safety
no fear or hurt

floating, all-knowing,
one with God
the highest vibration of song

gravity is history
no rules in ballet
glowing auras frolic with ease and grace

mighty, wise, serene
no threat, just bliss
looking down at myself but my body's not me

dancing with death   9

earthly whispers plead
grieving, suffering, bargaining
for a homeless soul's return

surrendered to telepathic music
reduced to five senses
a thrust dims the light

inhaling, exhaling
beating to my heart's drum
a different reunion fills it with joy

a story to tell
a survivor's showcase
melodic temptation to reenter the gates

retracing the trip
to that blinding glimpse
tapping into the hope of luminous eternity

aching aging body
soul's dancing partner in crime
blood circulation, mortal organs resound

wounds, scars, soul stains
feet firm on the floor
yearning for heaven, my true ballroom... my
home.

This is the sacred story of experiencing the after-life. Life often feels so painful, that whether you have experienced death or not, the thought of "resting in heavenly peace" can be such a strong pull.

What are simple, easy ways in which you could create peace and rest in your life?

_____

_____

_____

_____

_____

_____

_____

_____

_____

_____

_____

dancing alone

you walk across the floor
our eyes lock
take my hand - you say
and I can't say no

you lead
and I trust
I follow each step
wear a blindfold

intoxicated in your sweat
slow tempo
bolero slow death

the crowd's gone
it's you and me
souls swaying, burning heat

intense tango
toxic crush
fast beats, adrenaline rush

spinning violently
losing control
suffocating, yet I need more

bruised body, drained sole
no grace, no space,
faint pulse

hitting the ground
exhausted, afraid
guilt, shame,
embarrassed to seek aid

press pause
charm-sober
put one foot after the other

labored breathing
trembling, trying
rehearse a new routine
balance while crying

dancing alone
spacious empty room
merengue, bachata
salsa, cumbia tunes

my world is my stage
not falling anymore
enjoying my moves
stay across the floor

dancing with death

The story of recovery from codependency, trauma bonds, and fantasy bonds has been a recurring pattern in my life.

If you have been in toxic relationships, give yourself grace for not seeing what you could not yet see, and for not knowing what you did not yet know. You can now choose a different path.

What patterns do you want to stop in your personal relationships?

_____

_____

_____

_____

_____

_____

_____

_____

_____

_____

stages

say it isn't so
can't face the music
it's not real, no

rhythm fury, clenched fist
adieu jazz fingers
composure's adrift

clumsy feet are to blame
I'll do anything, promise
just take the pain away

deep tomb to bury my faith
demons move closer
hope skips away

little black dress
time to weep
be still, be plain

no fancy dance gear
days of luto
no place for cheer

sacred gathering inside
moving eulogy
loud sobs, and cries

dancing with death

light foot-tapping, gentle nods
grief dances away
to rock and hip pop

demi-pointe shoes, light red dress
let go ceremony
celebrate what's left

According to Elisabeth Kübler-Ross, there are 5 stages in grieving: shock and denial, anger, bargaining, depression, and acceptance. Each stage is natural and necessary in processing a loss. Think of both recent and past losses and list ones that you have yet to process.

How can you honor yourself and commit to go through the stages of grief that you have not fully experienced?

_____

_____

_____

_____

_____

_____

_____

_____

_____

_____

_____

paradoxical two-step

everything rots and dies
death is unavoidable

everyone's fate is the grave
death is inevitable

death is everywhere around you
death is inescapable

you can die anytime any moment
death is unpredictable

whether in the womb, youth, or old age
death is on time

in the fiercest of real or perceived wars
death is honorable

as we anticipate the main event
death is an usher

in the midst of chaos and cries
death is serene

for the ying needs the yang
death is truly reasonable

since the alpha and through the omega
death is unceasing

dancing with death

in a world of faux and lies
death is natural

though the modern-age discoveries
death is unexplainable

the villain on every stage,
death is misunderstood

a refined and cultured dancer
death is pure grace

a reward for the heroic
death is spiritual

just like the seasonal dance
death is temporary

mortals fear unknown sounds
death is courageous

prance beyond the veil of Earth
death is a doorway

because the soul is immortal
death is divine

if it's born, it's to die
death is part of life

dancing with death   19

Death is a natural process in the context of life, and yet, there is such stigma around it. We find ourselves fearing and resisting what we cannot change, cannot control, and is certain to happen.

How can you increase your sense of acceptance around death?

_____

_____

_____

_____

_____

_____

_____

_____

_____

_____

_____

morbid revue

staring at the gravesite
they've said their goodbyes
casket's 6 feet under
there my body lies

but I must confess
I've been dying all the while
every day dies at night
we live in such denial

every morning, every eve
one part of us dies
we pretend it's not aging
call it growing - foolish lies

flowers die
vase or field
just like the wishes
we've long concealed

birds will pass on
sky or ground
just like hope
by hurt is drowned

waves die out
the river's dry
just like dreams
dumped to comply

dancing with death

seasons change
their essence fades
love stories fail
though love may remain

insects squashed
merciless death
innocence dies
with each human breath

in forest hunting
dying's a sport
long lives our ego
though life is short

all mammals perish
and return to dust
our talents and gifts
wear out and rust

the fish in the ocean
die or get caught
and so do ideas
when carried out not

trees turn to snags
and fruits do rot
like plants, people wither
like it or not

but staring at the gravesite
I do not shed tears or weep
for all of my memories
I forever will keep

though it all seems to cease
our souls never will
dancing for all eternity
all bliss, joy, and thrill

our beauty and goodness
forever endure
no life expectancy
earth's just a detour

reading my tombstone
now awake and wise
all illusions gone
with my earthly eyes

We are limitless beings living a limited
life experience. Therefore, our view of
death can, at times, be shortsighted. We
focus on the aging, illness, and death of
the body, while our souls are endless and
everlasting.

How would you describe death from an eternal
perspective?

_____

_____

_____

_____

_____

_____

_____

_____

_____

_____

_____

organ recital

if my body is my temple
a den of robbers must be
corrupted with trapped trauma
overturned by disease

butterflies in my stomach
racy heart, weak knees
giant lump in my throat
is it fight, flight, or freeze?

frowning, shallow breath
lungs are coal
resigned, turning blue,
slumped, sorrowed soul

liver's not one who lives
no flow, blockage, high shrieks
grrrr, heavy sweat
bitter eyes, reddish cheeks

dilated pupils
kidney threatened
anxious, shrinking, shaky legs
danger reckoned

nightmares,
night sweats
vivid memories,
restlessness

dancing with death

hole in my gut
muscles tense
brain is absent
flashbacks dead intense

hands tied
bent out of shape
with them I'm trapped
no way to escape

Just like our emotions can be found and felt in our bodies, our unprocessed pain can be stored in our organs, tissues, skin, muscles and endocrine glands.

What emotions or events could you process to contribute to better holistic health?

_____

_____

_____

_____

_____

_____

_____

_____

_____

_____

_____

_____

_____

embrace

don't fear death
fear wandering meaninglessly
wasting precious time
second guessing yourself
fear not loving, not learning
fear living a lie

don't hate death
hate unrealistic standards
your expectations of perfect
and endless questioning of your worth
hate injustice and prejudice
and the comparison joint

don't blame death
blame the cookie, the couch
your choice of toxic sedation
and the boundaries you don't set
blame the yeses you don't mean
and the nos you don't say

don't shame death
shame the inner voice that judges you
shame the urge to hide your truth
and don't make yourself small
shame the sense of false humility
and the dulling of your shine

don't condemn death
condemn the quiet hesitation
to live be your limitless self
to use your voice, dance your song
condemn what blocks your joy
and sabotages your possibilities

don't fear, hate, blame
don't shame, don't condemn death
for death's just a transition
a state change, a sweet release
your imminent fate
your home, a house of joy, love, and peace

Fear, hatred, blame, shame, and condemnation all have a place in our life experience. However, we often misdirect them or use them inappropriately.

What are some proper events and experiences toward which you could direct this energy?

_____

_____

_____

_____

_____

_____

_____

_____

_____

_____

_____

_____

invalidated Ballerina

Little Ballerina
don't you cry
soon, you'll be dancing
soon, you'll be fine

Little Ballerina
you must be sleeping
don't stay up all night
in useless weeping

Little Ballerina
have gratitude
you get to confront
he who did this to you

Little Ballerina
the same happened to me
and I'm dancing now
weee! just look at me

Little Ballerina
from this, you'll learn
everything happens for a reason
it works out in turn

Little Ballerina
you were born to dance
you're not a quitter
so, relax your stance

dancing with death

Little Ballerina
others have moved on
and you're a strong one
go and dance to your song

Little Ballerina
it could be worse
you're still alive
let's just rehearse

Little Ballerina
what you should do
is forget it ever happened
and your dreams pursue

Little Ballerina
life's not really fair
chin up, dainty dancer
don't complain, don't swear

Little Ballerina
you're so sensitive, weak
that's a little dramatic
maybe smile, and look sweet

Little Ballerina
be responsible, miss
you control your thoughts
I know you've got this

dancing with death

Little Ballerina
I'm suffering too
I can't bear the thought
of this happening to you

Little Ballerina
this always happens to you
I think it is time
that you look for a clue

Little Ballerina
that wasn't too bright
try not to get hurt
maybe put up a fight

Little Ballerina
are you sure of these facts
did you misunderstand
and insanely react?

Little Ballerina
it's been a while
time to get over it
move on, my child

Many well-meaning fellow-travelers in our life journey invalidate our experience either by dismissing our pain or encouraging us to bypass it with motivational guilt. Rather than bringing healing, these words can poke wounds and bring deep shame. As we learn that validation must come from within, we are freed from our perceived need for others' approval, acceptance, and appreciation, and we let go of toxic and poisonous interactions.

What are some steps you can take to actively validate yourself?

_____

_____

_____

_____

_____

_____

_____

_____

_____

a victim's ballad

I was murdered that day
though you think I'm alive

I jumped off the edge
when I got in that car

he stabbed my faith to death
useless was my fight

overdosed in his hatred
I still feel it inside

yes, he drowned all my hope
with his horrific acts

he shot all my dreams
and wishes goodbye

and he poisoned my joy
all I've got left is cries

he choked out my trust
for all of mankind

his words, dehydrating,
for mercy I was starved

he crashed at me head on
and my innocence died

he burned my possibilities
I'm a zombie day and night

diseased all my thoughts
with his heinous desire

lethal touch electrocuted
all my body and mind

he took my life, my breath
though judged not as homicide

and shame slits my wrists
I'm a corpse, realize

I jumped in front of a train
when I escaped the crime

After two decades hiding this experience, I shared a detailed account on my blog and titled it "The Story I Never Wanted to Share." In this poem, I explore the different ways to physically die, and point out the preciousness of what is buried along with the pain, as we walk around living a flatlined existence.

What is the story you've never wanted to share? What may come back to life when you own that story?

_____

_____

_____

_____

_____

_____

_____

_____

_____

_____

I'm dancing yet

making a choice I could regret
one more Earthly dance yet

going back to the unknown
to see what I didn't see yet

returning to uncertainty
to do what I didn't do yet

saying yes to suffering
just to say what I didn't say yet

risking it all for a chance
to become what I didn't become yet

giving the best up
to give what I didn't give yet

bid goodbye to the highest wisdom
to learn what I didn't learn yet

sacrificing inner calm
to feel what I didn't feel yet

heeding the voice that says "not your time"
the word I most dreaded: YET

dancing with death

This is the story of coming back to life on Earth after experiencing Heaven. It is also the story of making the conscious choice to stay alive when it feels like the wrong one.

Share what you've got yet to learn, experience, feel, say, do, give, and discover as you're in this plane and stage?

_____

_____

_____

_____

_____

_____

_____

_____

_____

_____

_____

_____

dancing with death

solo to symphony

out of the darkness
into the blinding light
comforting presence
golden peace divine

not winged and faceless,
weightless and wise
they see me, they hear me
sweet beings of light

I feel free and pure
I am unafraid
piercing frequencies hit
like a love serenade

I'm embraced, I'm enlightened
fully accepted as me
holy messengers singing
of my divinity

glowing personages
soothing fire
holy realm, matchless beauty
luminescent attire

white open windows
wide open doors
penetrating fragrances
endless resplandor

sacred encounters
no longer alone
angelic guardians
help me feel at home

emanating real love
spiritual guides
intense vivid colors
here where God abides

ministering angels
telekinetic bright souls
telepathic partners
my essence show whole

virtues, miracles
and blessings abound
in this quiet journey
my true self I found

soft vibration of glory
radiant entities' embrace
purple energy surrounds me
in this heavenly space

out of the light
I have returned
but forget I must not
what I there learned

limitless possibilities
we are one family
not otherness but oneness
for all eternity

The best way to describe what I remember from my out-of-body experience: the beauty, the joy, and the oneness.

Separation, "otherness," and segregation are illusions. Competition and comparison are traps. The way we create Heaven on Earth is by becoming ONE.

What are some little ways in which you can create integration, connection, and unification within yourself and with the people in your life?

_____

_____

_____

_____

_____

_____

_____

_____

_____

_____

slow dance

unconscious, but I can hear the music
breathless, but the lyrics still touch my
soul

traveling gently to the point of no return
irregular beating, heart's rhythm's off

spinning in circles, dizzy circulation,
no appetites on the bright lit floor

body's sweating, feet cold
hanging on to something before I let go

air's heavy, mouth's dry
feeling restless, mind body and soul

ICU madness
half truths are told

fixed pupils, flat line
heart at a standstill, no oxygen flow

eyelids half-open, pale skin
muscles relaxing, song's going hush

body still, brain's done
cells deteriorating in unison

dancing with death

news official
certificate signed, flowers bought

deceased, but I can sing and sway
goodbye, take my liver and kidney and move on

lonely cemetery, empty grave
my bones are there, but my spirit's gone

The story of a dying body. Every organ and system slows down to allow for a more vivid spiritual aliveness. We can consciously pause and unplug from busyness. By creating daily moments of calm, we can connect with our divinity.

What are some easy actions you can take to be more present and feel more alive?

_____

_____

_____

_____

_____

_____

_____

_____

_____

_____

_____

performance critic

you're doing it wrong
not conforming to the rules
wandering through life with no form

are you paying attention?
try at least a little harder…
what a lousy presentation!

slouched posture, zero grace
look in the mirror
wipe the fear off your face

stand up straighter, puny one
deficient figures
unattractive body line

your whole shape needs improvement
your ugly appearance
matches your movement

can't stand your poor foot action
and how disgraceful
your distraction

a great rhythm, still you're off
never smooth
never enough

bad timing, catch your breath
your dance partner
should be Death

Jay Earley, Ph.D. and Bonnie Weiss, LCSW, identified seven types of inner critics: the perfectionist, the taskmaster, the inner controller, the guilt tripper, the destroyer, the underminer, and the molder or conformist. These voices come from outdated beliefs that seek to keep us safe, and instead, prevent us from seeing the beauty around and within.

Which of these critics speak to you? What do they say? How are they trying to help?

_____

_____

_____

_____

_____

_____

_____

_____

_____

_____

last dance

no one's invited to my rebirth
no death shower to celebrate

no one's chosen a playlist
no fancy gear, no photoshoot

no one wants to talk about it
no death plan has been devised

no one says you look ready
no advice for this new stage

no one's excited at the signs
no death classes to attend

no one's made up a go-home plan
no hospital tour has been set

no one wants to witness the end
no books for me on what to expect

no one's secured a doula
no death partner in my last dance

no one's holding out their cries
no tears from me as I become Light

What if we were to consciously prepare for death as we prepare for birth? What if we treated death with honor, reverence, and awe? If you pondered on today's date, you'd realize that it is the last day of its kind you will ever live.

"Memento Mori," is Latin for "remember that you must die." What would you do differently if each new calendar date acted as a reminder of the inevitability of your death?

_____

_____

_____

_____

_____

_____

_____

_____

_____

_____

_____

the temptress

in the quiet darkness of my room
Death penetrates my brain
and tells me I am hers

her words intoxicate me
as she reminds me of my shame
her mystery lures and tempts me

sweet evil whispers, she calls to me
my psyche is hypnotized with doubt
and I want to indulge in her essence

my heart races with excitement
her enticing dance with ghosts of my past
her dark pull is irresistible

her embrace feels warm
I am cold and alone
and I am weaker in her presence

her seductive gaze draws me
as wicked thoughts
flirt with my fear

I succumb to her
and the burdens of my living
fill my senses and awareness

dancing with death

Death casts her spell
and I want to lay with her
a promise to strip out of all regrets

I surrender to her sway
I begin to plan our sweet escape
from my unworthy existence

I slowly walk with her
and our arms entangle and I feel safe
finally a place to belong

she taunts me with her moves
her twisted passion is magical
and hopeless, I lose control

"take me" I urge her
I am lost in her deep lust
unlovable I'll be no more

our connection is electric
low vibration, high intensity
I have a voice, Death feels like home

fascinating, alluring, forbidden
she's taken over my senses
I'm her captive yet free of the torment we
call life

dancing with death

Death is charming, she's enchanting
I'm magnetized and attracted
and thoughts of her invade me day and
night

as I hear the sound of silence
suddenly back from my trance
our encounter is no longer and I yearn for
our next dance

The contemplation of suicide does not feel like a crisis… The intense seduction of death is so deceiving that ending life can feel like the only safe and sound solution to all problems and pains. Having a plan to resist her woo will be helpful in assuring you will decline the invitation when she's most insisting.

Write a list of what you can do before, during and after being under her influence.

_____

_____

_____

_____

_____

_____

_____

_____

_____

_____

_____

unrest

unfinished projects
some bring nostalgia, the others relief

unpaid bills
this one stings, feeling the guilt

unsaid words
would it have mattered, in the long run?

unkempt space
better clear up your clutter first

unstable affairs
documents, policies, plans up in the air

unasked questions
arrangements to make, conflicting
suggestions

unclaimed possessions
beneficiaries quarreling with sad obsession

unassigned tasks
they're left with the burden of who's
doing what

unexpected costs
I'll be a burden even when I go

undue pressure
the impact on them I can never measure

uncertain decisions
distraught family, dispositions

uncharted journey
somewhat familiar but really unknown

unprocessed pain, unfair delay
I'll dance with death, just not today

I'm grateful I've decided to stay alive out of guilt, shame, and impending regret. But fear-based decisions are not sustainable in the long term.

What love-based reasons to stay alive can you think of? What do you love about being in this earthly realm? What would you love to yet experience?

_____

_____

_____

_____

_____

_____

_____

_____

_____

_____

_____

interlude

this act is exhausting
the characters cold
the plot terrifying

all this drama is draining me
fatigued, hollow
sapped energy, muscles weak

mask is heavy, costume tight
no trust or dignity
just this script of lies recite

want to get off this stage
fall into a deep sleep
numb the inevitable rage

longing for a second act
Impatient, restless
though transition is a fact

be mindful to the cast
the audience
expects a blast

the tears and despair are real
the sweet afterlife
sounds ideal

I hate this recurring role
exactness and precision
it all takes a toll

co-stars are demons and ghosts
this tragedy is unbearable
and I'm tired of the notes

more fame and more glory
when I'm finally offstage
they'll actually care for my story

the first act comes to an end
time for the eternal play
where I don't have to pretend

Many of us learned that we had to suppress our emotions and hide our authentic self in order to survive. We make decisions that are driven by outdated beliefs and unconscious dynamics that no longer serve us and that prevent both our humanity and divinity to be expressed.

What is one tiny habit you can implement in your life that will allow you to further align with your true self?

_____

_____

_____

_____

_____

_____

_____

_____

_____

_____

misplaced move

victimhood is not a mentality
it's being through cruel brutality

victimhood is making sense of the world
when its atrocities have come unfurled

victimhood is a haunting song
saying "you're broken, you don't belong"

victimhood is altered brain chemistry
there's no safety, no serenity

victimhood is not self-inflicted
but an outraged cry from the afflicted

victimhood is being robbed
of innocence, identity fogged

victimhood is a sharp sword
when your misstep inflicts remorse

victimhood is a lethal state
when you didn't chose that dreadful fate

victimhood is feeling a tragic loss
while others witness it and scoff

dancing with death

victimhood is not about pity
it's ruins, shackles, it's not pretty

victimhood is being hurt
something that words cannot revert

victimhood is not crippling stance
it's in the choreography of this dance

It's natural to feel like a victim when you have been victimized. Your emotions are valid. Emotions are neither good nor bad; neither positive nor negative. Emotions shine a bright light into what is happening inside of us. Rather than fighting the messenger, it's best to allow yourself to process the news.

How would embracing and honoring all your emotions serve you? Write at least three outcomes for each meaningful area of your life.

_____

_____

_____

_____

_____

_____

_____

_____

center stage

it's showtime
tight throat, sweaty palms
the anxiety kicks in

it shouldn't be daunting
they say
but there's so much noise within

a true performer
wouldn't have stage fright
this panic attack is a sin

the pep talks
don't really work
I'm uncomfortable in my skin

and so I show up to life
I love to dance
but I tremble at every spin

no warm up's long enough
to keep balance
and avoid the traumatic injuries

when I fall
I feel uneasy
knowing all eyes are on me

get up, smile
keep on dancing
make eye contact, lift your chin

I feel vulnerable,
want to run
but they don't seem to take a hint

"the show must go on"
relax
we all came here to be seen

so I suppress
I move on
no matter how hurt I've been

cool down period's too short
another dreaded show
will very soon begin

must be normal
or you'll be judged
prove you can really fit in

falling apart
scared to say no
dry mouth, weak in the knees

but I'm too depressed to dance
if I don't cry it out
I'll fall ill

embarrassed, hide in the back
hesitant steps
tears of anger down my cheeks

invisible dancer
no longer offensive
one day I'll dance at my own beat

Your body, your mind, and your soul are constantly sending you signals of what truly aligns with your life's purpose. As much as you can, look and listen beyond the impossible and unreasonable standards to perform. As much as possible, look and listen within for answers on what life would be like if you didn't feel like you had to always perform and put on a show.

What is something you could do in the direction of what gives you life… while honoring your pace?

_____

_____

_____

_____

_____

_____

_____

_____

_____

keep on dancing

I want to celebrate you for joining me on this adventure, and to invite you to greet yourself with deep love and gratitude for your courageous and curious heart.

As you continue dancing with death, may you remember to be kind to yourself. Just like birth, death is a step in the choreography of our eternal existence.

Your journey in this book doesn't end here. Pick it up again when thoughts of life and death feel overwhelming. Read a poem out loud. Allow yourself to lean into the pain, be still, and intentionally study it with all your being.

Processing your painful thoughts, beliefs, and experiences will help you achieve Emotional Wholeness.

When you are ready, write your own story, create something that will outlive your mortal journey. Create something real. Resist the filters. Bring on the hatred, the struggles, the grief, and all the dark shadows.

And if you feel the urge, share it with others, because it is through our vulnerable stories that we create a ripple effect of self-acceptance, peace, and freedom.

Lastly, I want to remind you that you are equally lovable when you're in the spotlight, shining your precious light, as you are when immersed in the darkest deepest shadows.

You matter… no matter what.

BE Positive On Your Own Terms,

Elayna

44761603R00049